THE SCIENCE OF A BRIDGE COLLAPSE

NIKOLE BROOKS BETHEA

Published in the United States of America by Cherry Lake Publishing
Ann Arbor, Michigan
www.cherrylakepublishing.com

Consultants: C. C. Fu, Director and Research Professor, Department of Civil and Environmental Engineering, University of Maryland; Marla Conn, ReadAbility, Inc.
Editorial direction: Red Line Editorial
Book design and illustration: Design Lab

Photo Credits: Shutterstock Images, cover, 1, 9 (left), 13, 18; US Coast Guard, 5; Alex Ghidan/Shutterstock Images, 9 (right); Fernando Blanco Calzada/Shutterstock Images, 10; AP Images, 15; Paul Sakuma/AP Images, 17; Robert A. Mansker/Shutterstock Images, 21; Weaver Tripp/St. Petersburg Times/AP Images, 27; Delmas Lehman, 28

Library of Congress Cataloging-in-Publication Data
  Bethea, Nikole Brooks, author.
  The science of a bridge collapse / by Nikole Brooks Bethea.
     pages cm. -- (Disaster science)
  Audience: Age 11.
  Audience: Grades 4 to 6.
  Includes bibliographical references and index.
  ISBN 978-1-63137-623-8 (hardcover) -- ISBN 978-1-63137-668-9 (pbk.) -- ISBN 978-1-63137-713-6 (pdf ebook) -- ISBN 978-1-63137-758-7 (hosted ebook)
  1. Bridge failures--Juvenile literature. 2. Bridges--Accidents--Juvenile literature. I. Title.

  TG470.B45 2015
  624.2--dc23   2014004029

Cherry Lake Publishing would like to acknowledge the work of The Partnership for 21st Century Skills. Please visit www.p21.org for more information.

Printed in the United States of America
Corporate Graphics Inc.
July 2014

ABOUT THE AUTHOR

Nikole Brooks Bethea is a professional engineer and a writer. She holds a bachelor's and a master's degree in environmental engineering from the University of Florida. She lives in the Florida Panhandle with her husband and four sons.

TABLE OF CONTENTS

CHAPTER 1

A DISASTROUS DESIGN

Bridges are everywhere. They allow people to easily cross railways, waterways, highways, and low areas such as valleys or canyons. Bridges are so common people often cross them without even thinking about them. They assume the structures were designed properly. But sometimes bridges fail.

On the evening of August 1, 2007, in Minneapolis, Minnesota, the unthinkable happened. Tom Hughes was driving his pickup truck across the Interstate 35W

Bridge when he felt an unusual movement. Ripples in the roadway seemed to move toward him. His truck bumped over them. Something was wrong. He decided to stomp on the accelerator, trying to get off the bridge as quickly as possible. Suddenly, he felt the back of his truck drop. The truck fell through the air and tumbled down the collapsing bridge. It finally landed on a piece

The collapse left dozens of cars scattered on the remains of the structure.

of the broken bridge. Hughes managed to escape with a broken vertebrae and wrist. Other people on the bridge that day were not so fortunate.

About half of the 1,907-foot (581 m) bridge crossing the Mississippi River had collapsed. More than 450 feet (137 m) of it dropped into the river. Traffic was heavy, and there had been 111 vehicles traveling on that part of the bridge. Thirteen people died in the collapse. Another 145 people were injured.

The bridge had opened in 1967, and about 141,000 vehicles crossed it daily. What went wrong on this particular day? How could such a disaster be prevented from happening again? These were the questions the **engineers** working with the National Transportation Safety Board (NTSB) needed to answer. They closely examined the conditions on the bridge before the disaster.

On the day of the accident, construction work was happening on the bridge. Four of the eight traffic lanes were closed. Just two lanes were open in each direction.

Earlier in the day, construction equipment and materials had been stored in two of the closed lanes. The stored materials, equipment, and workers weighed 578,735 pounds (262,510 kg). The vehicles traveling on the bridge weighed another 121,750 pounds (55,225 kg). Engineers worked to find out whether this had been too much weight for the bridge to hold.

Officials ran computer models for the bridge design. These models showed the bridge should have been able to safely hold the combined weight of the construction equipment and vehicles. The investigation continued.

Bridge pieces were pulled from the river. They were laid out on the ground in their original positions for inspection. Reviews by engineers showed problems with the gusset plates, pieces of metal that connect two steel beams. The plates were 0.5 inches (1.3 cm) thick, but they should have been 1 inch (2.5 cm) thick. In November 2008, the NTSB released a report concluding that the cause of the collapse was this design error.

The engineers' findings showed that transportation officials did not study designs for planned bridges closely enough to catch errors. They found that the review process for designs needed improvement.

The Interstate 35W Bridge collapsed because of design errors. It's important to know that this kind of problem is very rare. Most bridge collapses are caused by external forces. These forces include natural disasters such as floods, hurricanes, and earthquakes.

TYPES OF BRIDGES

These diagrams show some major types of bridges, including beam, arch, truss, cantilever, cable-stayed, and suspension bridges. Do you see any of these kinds of bridges on a regular basis? Why do you think the bridges you see have one design instead of another?

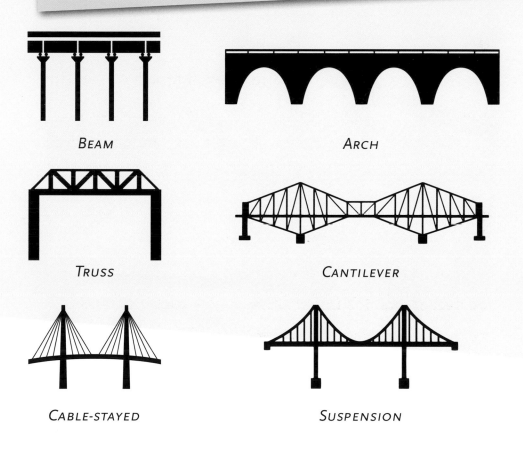

BEAM

ARCH

TRUSS

CANTILEVER

CABLE-STAYED

SUSPENSION

Simply putting too much weight on a bridge can bring it down as well. Finally, crashes of boats or large trucks can also result in collapses. In the field of forensic study, scientists and engineers examine the forces and designs involved in collapses to prevent future disasters from occurring.

Bridge designers apply lessons from collapses when planning and building new bridges.

The Importance of Bridge Inspection

The Silver Bridge collapsed into the Ohio River in 1967. It fell because a crack developed in a piece of the structure called an eyebar. The tragedy killed 46 people. The US Congress began the National Bridge Inspection Program the next year. Now bridges are inspected every two years. Accurate reports are crucial to successful bridge inspection programs. Inspectors must record detailed data. These reports become a lifetime record of the bridge. They help engineers know how the bridge's condition changes over time. Engineers use the reports to determine if repairs are needed to keep the bridge safe.

Many tools are used to inspect and maintain bridges. Scrapers and brushes clean bridge surfaces. Special equipment removes small pieces of concrete or wood for testing. Tools that measure heat and sound check for hollow spots below the bridge surface. Steel thickness is determined with special devices that can take accurate measurements. These devices include micrometers, calipers, and ultrasonic gages.

CHAPTER 2

COLLAPSE BY SCOUR

One of the biggest reasons for bridge collapses is known as scour. It happens when the soil around a bridge's foundation washes away. The condition is usually caused by quickly flowing water, and it is common during flooding.

Bridges are supported by columns called piers. When piers are placed in a river, they block the flow of some of the water. Engineers call this reducing the bridge's cross-sectional area. When the same amount of water flows through a smaller space, it moves faster. The faster

Bridges crossing rivers must be designed with the dangers of scour in mind.

flowing water washes away the soil around the piers. It can even create a hole in the soil around the bottom of the pier. If the pier sinks into this hole, it cannot properly support the bridge. The bridge is then at an increased risk of collapsing.

What happened to the Schoharie Creek Bridge in New York is an example of scour causing collapse. On April 5, 1987, the National Weather Service issued flood warnings for Amsterdam, New York, because of heavy rainfall. Water in Schoharie Creek had been rising since the previous day. Suddenly, two **spans** of the bridge fell into the creek. An hour and a half later, another span collapsed. Four cars and one large truck fell into the creek, killing 10 people.

The bridge wreckage was pulled from the creek after the flood. Studies showed scour around two of the bridge piers. Engineers discovered the bridge was also missing something: riprap. Riprap is rock or concrete placed around the piers to protect them. The Schoharie Creek Bridge

THE TANGIWAI DISASTER

Scour usually happens gradually. But sometimes, dramatic cases of scour can happen in just a few moments. In 1953, a hidden lake within a volcano in Tangiwai, New Zealand, suddenly flooded and spilled out through a cave. As the water flowed down the mountain, it picked up volcanic ash and boulders. The force of the water and debris smashed a bridge in the valley below, damaging several piers. Sadly, a train heading toward the bridge could not stop in time. The bridge collapsed and 151 people died.

disaster demonstrated the importance of underwater inspection of bridges. It also showed the importance of riprap in preventing scour collapses. A similar flood occurred at this bridge in 1955 without causing damage. At that time, the riprap was in place. It wore away in later years and was not replaced.

Sometimes installing riprap does not solve the scour problem. Instead, the underwater foundation must be changed. The concrete bases that piers sit on may need to be rebuilt. Making the bases bigger or deeper makes the bridge stronger.

Scour can happen slowly, but as the Schoharie Creek Bridge demonstrated, its effects can be devastating.

CHAPTER 3

OVERLOADING BRIDGES

To design a bridge, engineers must know the load it will carry. The dead load is the weight of the bridge structure itself and anything attached to it. Before it can carry anything, a bridge must be able to support its own weight. The dead load includes small things such as signs and railings. It also includes large, heavy things such as roads or railroad tracks. Sidewalks and water pipes are more examples of dead loads. The dead load is permanent.

The live load is the weight of the cars, trucks, trains, or pedestrians passing over a bridge. A live load is temporary and moves along the bridge. Engineers calculate the total load a bridge must hold. They determine how the load affects each of the large pieces of the bridge, called members. Members include beams and columns.

Two major kinds of forces act on bridge members: **compression** and **tension**. Compression pushes or

On one day in 1987, the Golden Gate Bridge in San Francisco, California, was opened to pedestrians only. Crowds put a huge live load on the bridge.

squeezes the members, while tension pulls or stretches them. Some members are better at handling compression, while others are designed to withstand tension. These forces keep bridges balanced. However, sometimes a force causes a bridge beam to **deflect**, or bend. For example, the weight of too many vehicles on a bridge might bend a beam. There is compression on one side of the beam and tension on the other.

TEAMWORK IN DESIGNING BRIDGES

Designing a bridge is not a job for one person. It takes teamwork. Experts from many different fields help design each bridge. **Geotechnical** engineers study the foundation. The strongest bridges in the world are worthless if their foundations will not support them. **Hydrologic** and **hydraulic** engineers study how a bridge will change the flow of a river. They aim to design bridges that prevent scour. These engineers also study how normal water flow and floods will affect a bridge and surrounding areas. Structural engineers design the bridge structure itself. They determine how strong the concrete and steel must be to support the traffic flow. Roadway engineers design the roads that cross over and under bridges. They also make sure rainwater will drain off the road in the right direction. This is called stormwater design. Also important to the team are contractors and inspectors. They make sure plans are followed in the construction of a bridge. This ensures the bridge is built according to the engineers' design.

CHAPTER 4

ENVIRONMENTAL FORCES

Natural disasters such as hurricanes, volcanoes, and earthquakes can also weaken bridge structures. Weather such as wind, rain, and ice can also lead to collapses. Just like live loads, environmental forces are temporary loads on bridges. Unfortunately, bridges sometimes cannot hold up to these short-lived forces.

Hurricanes bring strong winds and high tides. This often proves disastrous for bridges. The cost to rebuild Gulf Coast bridges damaged by 2004's Hurricane Ivan

Hurricane Katrina badly damaged the Biloxi Bay Bridge in Biloxi, Mississippi.

and 2005's Hurricane Katrina has been more than
$1 billion. During Hurricane Katrina, two bridges on
US Highway 90 in Mississippi collapsed. The Interstate
10 Bridge connecting New Orleans and Slidell,
Louisiana, also collapsed.

Damage to bridges from earthquakes is caused by
ground motion. The length of time the ground vibrates

CORROSION IN STEEL BRIDGES

The environment can damage steel bridges. Moisture, heat, oxygen, and salt cause steel to corrode, or be eaten away. Rust is a sign of **corrosion**. When steel corrodes, the bridge is weakened. Corrosion can lead to bridge collapses. Special coatings are painted on steel bridges to prevent corrosion. The coatings protect the steel from the harmful effects of the environment.

affects the amount of damage. California is particularly vulnerable to earthquakes. The state sits on a line called the San Andreas Fault where huge pieces of Earth's surface slide against one another underground. This movement causes earthquakes. In the afternoon of October 17, 1989, the Loma Prieta earthquake struck the San Francisco Bay Area of California. A 250-ton (230 metric ton) portion of the San Francisco–Oakland Bay Bridge's upper deck collapsed onto the lower deck of this two-level truss bridge.

The bridge was repaired, but engineers went to work designing a better bridge. On September 2, 2013, a new East Span of the Bay Bridge opened. This state-of-the-art suspension bridge is designed to withstand extremely powerful earthquakes. Hinge pipe beams are a new technology used in the bridge. The centers of these beams absorb the earthquake's energy, protecting the rest of the bridge. Afterward, if they are damaged, the centers of the beams can be replaced. Sensors are installed throughout the new bridge to record ground movement. The measurements are sent to scientists for study.

DESIGN STANDARDS

On the morning of February 9, 1971, the San Fernando earthquake hit California. The highway overpass at the **interchange** of Interstate 5 and Interstate 14 collapsed. In response to the bridge failure, the government began researching bridge design standards for earthquakes. In 1983, the nation's first earthquake design guidelines for bridges were adopted.

Floating ice around the piers of a bridge can also cause collapse. One example of this occurred at Falls View Bridge. This bridge was located below Niagara Falls and was a popular tourist attraction. On the night of January 25, 1938, an ice jam formed against the bridge. Ice began forming and blocked the water. By the next afternoon, ice had piled up 50 feet (15 m) higher than the normal water level. Pressure kept growing against the bridge's structure. The next day, the ice tore Falls View Bridge from its foundation. The bridge collapsed into the river. An unusual act of nature caused this collapse. It is not always possible to design for these extreme situations. Scientists and engineers must try to plan for any disaster or weather event that could hit the bridges they design.

GALLOPING GERTIE

The Tacoma Narrows Bridge is one of the most-studied failures in bridge engineering. The suspension bridge opened in Washington in July 1940. It was nicknamed "Galloping Gertie" because it moved in the wind.

At about 7:00 a.m. on November 7, 1940, the bridge began violently twisting in the wind. Around 11:00 a.m. the bridge fell into the water. The authorities launched an investigation that is a great example of the steps of the scientific method. **Observation** was the first step of the investigation. The twisting and collapse of the bridge had been filmed, so there was footage to review. The next step was to develop a **hypothesis**. Engineers believed wind had caused the collapse. The idea had to be tested. The wind had been fairly light, blowing at 42 miles per hour (68 kmh). Wind effects on bridges were not well understood at the time.

Testing was the next step in understanding the bridge collapse. Models of the bridge were tested in wind tunnels. The final step in the investigation was explanation. The bridge's movement had thrown a supporting cable off the structure, throwing the bridge out of balance. Its existing up-and-down motion turned into a twisting motion. The bridge's narrow width, light weight, and flexibility were weaknesses in wind. Today, wind-tunnel testing is done on models of long-span bridges before they are built.

CHAPTER 5

COLLISIONS AND ACCIDENTS

Besides traffic flow, dead loads, and natural forces, bridge designers must take into account the risk of accidents. Vehicles and ships collide with bridges. These collisions are considered **sudden loads**.

The old Sunshine Skyway Bridge was a Florida truss bridge that collapsed after a ship hit it. On the morning of May 9, 1980, a ship called the *Summit Venture* was traveling from the Gulf of Mexico to the Port of Tampa Bay. The first part of the trip was foggy and rainy. Then suddenly, tropical-storm force winds battered the ship. The *Summit Venture*'s radar failed, preventing it from detecting obstacles through the weather. Rain poured down and the ship's captain could not see where the ship was going. The *Summit Venture* headed into a bend in the channel. Strong winds pushed it out of the correct path and toward a bridge.

By the time the captain saw the bridge, it was too late. He ordered the anchors dropped and reversed the engines to slow down. But the *Summit Venture* crashed into a pier. The pier fell, and

A huge portion of the Sunshine Skyway Bridge's roadway fell into the water when a ship collided with the structure.

The new Sunshine Skyway Bridge has a tall center section, allowing ships to safely pass beneath it.

Interstate 275 fell with it. A bus, six cars, and a pickup truck went into the water. Thirty-five people died.

When rebuilding the Sunshine Skyway Bridge, steps were taken to prevent future collisions. The new cable-stayed bridge opened in 1987. It is 25 feet (8 m) taller than the original bridge. This gives more room for ships to clear the bridge. Designers also moved the new

[21ST CENTURY SKILLS LIBRARY]

bridge farther away from the bend in the channel. The channel width at the new location is 1,000 feet (305 m), rather than the old measurement of 800 feet (244 m). This gave ships more room to pass between the bridge piers. Finally, the new piers are protected by 36 giant bumpers known as dolphins. They guard the piers by deflecting ships.

By studying bridge collapses of the past, engineers can design stronger bridges. Understanding factors such as scour, overloading, and environmental forces is important for the scientists, engineers, and designers who create future bridges.

Top Five Worst Bridge Collapses

1. **December 28, 1879**
   Tay Rail Bridge, Dundee, Scotland, 75 deaths. The wrong estimate of wind force was used in the design. The bridge collapsed during a storm, and a crossing train plummeted into the water.

2. **August 29, 1907**
   Quebec Bridge, Canada, 96 deaths (85 in first collapse and 11 in second collapse). The bridge first collapsed in 1907 after a member buckled during construction. The bridge was redesigned and collapsed again in 1916 as it was being lifted into place. It finally opened in December 1917.

3. **December 15, 1967**
   Silver Bridge, Ohio/West Virginia, 46 deaths. A defective eyebar on the suspension bridge cracked, causing it to collapse, carrying 37 vehicles along with it.

4. **May 9, 1980**
   Sunshine Skyway Bridge, Tampa Bay, Florida, 35 deaths. A freighter hit a pier during a storm, collapsing the bridge and sending a bus and seven other vehicles into the water.

5. **July 17, 1981**
   Hyatt Regency skywalks, Kansas City, Missouri, 114 deaths. Two overcrowded pedestrian bridges collapsed because of the weight of people and vibrations from their dancing.

LEARN MORE

FURTHER READING

Briscoe, Diana. *Bridge Building: Bridge Designs and How They Work.* Bloomington, MN: Red Brick Learning, 2005.

Hurley, Michael. *The World's Most Amazing Bridges.* Chicago, IL: Raintree, 2012.

WEB SITES

How Stuff Works—Top Ten Structurally Amazing Bridges
http://science.howstuffworks.com/engineering/structural/10-amazing-bridges.htm
Read about several bridges that make impressive use of engineering technology.

PBS—Building Big: Bridges
http://www.pbs.org/wgbh/buildingbig/bridge/index.html
This Web site includes interactive demonstrations of the forces, materials, and shapes that bridge engineers consider when building a new bridge.

GLOSSARY

compression (kuhm-PRESH-uhn) a force that pushes, squeezes, or presses

corrosion (kuh-ROH-zhun) the process of steel being worn away

deflect (di-FLEKT) to move out of place

engineers (en-juh-NIHRS) people who use math and science to build things and solve problems

geotechnical (jee-oh-TEK-nuh-kuhl) related to how rocks, soil, and minerals interact with engineered structures

hydraulic (hye-DRAW-lik) having to do with the behavior of moving or flowing water

hydrologic (hye-droh-LAW-jic) having to do with water

hypothesis (hye-POTH-uh-siss) an idea, or educated guess, that needs to be investigated

interchange (in-tur-CHAYNJ) a road intersection that often uses ramps to avoid crossing other lanes of traffic

observation (ob-zur-VAY-shuhn) information collected in a scientific investigation by using one's senses

spans (SPANS) sections of a bridge between neighboring supports

sudden loads (SUHD-uhn lohds) forces on a bridge that result from unexpected collisions

tension (TEN-shun) a force that pulls or stretches

INDEX